The NonSense of NonDual

by Liam Quirk

One Moon Press – Trenton NJ
Printed in USA
TheNonSenseOfNonDual.com

TABLE OF CONTENTS

1

POINTING AT THE MOON

The finger pointing at the moon doesn't matter.

The map is not the territory.

The word 'itself' has no meaning. No word has meaning.

Half empty or half full, the glass is just a container for what you want to drink. And if we are thirsty, we will find nothing to satisfy us.

I'd like to keep this as simple as possible. You cannot find what you are looking for. But that is not because it doesn't exist. If we seek something, it definitely exists. The problem is that what we seek may not be real. And if it is not real, we will never find it. It exists solely in our delusional longing, always a half-step out of reach. And if it *is* real, you will never find it. You can not ever find it because in seeking it you can't let go of what it is not. What you are not. The truth is that what is real must surprise you, sneak up on you like a flower hidden in the same place that you just looked.

If you are assuming that there is an intellectual definition of NonDual, you will be disappointed. NonDual is nonsensical. And it is so ordinary that you will probably not believe it when you also know it is happening. Especially not afterwards. That is what is so extraordinary about NonDual experience. It is so ordinary that we pass it by, give it a smug shrug. "This can't be it," we say to ourselves. And in naming it "it," we have already stepped out of it. We are conditioned to the unreal.

NonDual is the essential Both/And experience. The famous Rubin vase explains it best. We can see the vase, or the faces. Not both at the same time. That is a great analogy for consciousness itself. Awareness of self simultaneously creates awareness of other. You and I. It and me. Whatever.

Where there is "I," there is separation from what contains You and I. Of course the separation is not real. There can be no separation. That is our basic, essential delusion.

Delusion is not bad. Delusion is necessary.

Separation is a painful, ongoing choice. Yet we choose it because we need to. We can't recognize what is real yet. Pretending to make a different choice is an even deeper delusion. This kind of fruit will fall from the tree when it is ripe, not a moment before. It is much better not to try. Pretending to be ripe solidifies delusion until it must be broken, shattered into so many shards that they cannot all be found when we furiously try to piece them all back together. In the empty spaces that remain, hope is born, but hope must also ripen through letting go to what is real. Again and again and again. Eventually, hope reveals itself as faith.

The basic problem is duality. Yet even that word has no meaning. It is an abstraction from the reality of our flesh and bones. Better to stay close to the body to understand and experience the reality of duality. Better to wait, not to move at all until we begin to move spontaneously. Truly. That is NonDual.

2

ONE HAND CLAPPING

One answer to this Zen riddle is Om, the sound of the universe in being. One hand clapping is Oneness. It is so impossible that it almost hurts to imagine it. Yet calling it a sound is incorrect. It is a vibration. Sound is a specific experience of vibration. So when that tree falls in the woods where there is no one to hear it, there is still sound. And it is everywhere. You can still hear that vibration, ringing off the hook in every conch shell.

Oneness, another name for NonDual, is impossibly ridiculous. There is no funnier joke that you could ever tell. We should be running up to each other in the street, shaking each other by the shoulders and laughing at the impossibility of everything. Yet we are deadly serious. Just look at us on our morning commute. Or when we are at work. Dead serious. In the grocery store, too. Dead serious.

If you are living, Reality blows your mind in every moment. Everything else is dead. Sometimes Reality breaks through, and we catch someone's eye. We have to at least smile. We've been found out. We've been caught believing in our self importance. It feels good to know we can be real, if even for a moment. We have found eternal life.

So why is this so difficult? We are not yet flexible. We fear that if we entertain nonsense that something important will break. That is one of the funnier parts of the joke because if it can break, it is not important. Do you see that? What is true cannot be broken, so we should test everything. Put a hammer to it. Wail away. Pray for things to break. Then we will know where we stand.

This is not suggesting that we can be without pain. That is another popular chapter of delusion. The whole 'being without pain' trip. We run around like chumps, trying to be rid of pain. We do unspeakable things to others and to ourselves in the name of no pain. And when others are in obvious pain we close the door and say to ourselves and those we confide in that they must be doing something wrong. That pain is their own fault.

Ouch. That's harsh. When we don't understand something, we try to look and feel superior. Pain, pure and simply, is unrealized self. There is nothing more painful. That's the point. And this goes all the way up or all the way down, depending on how you like to look at it. All the way through to death. And to resurrection. But not to worry—you'll be back for another crack at it. So will I. We just need to remember that pain is not owned. It cannot be possessed. It is something else for us to surrender to, and to let go of. But not because we believe it will then somehow go away.

And here's another important point in this regard: we are afraid to discover who we really are. We prefer our familiar pain to the unknown pain up ahead. But not forever and always. One day we wake up suprised, and something is different. We suddenly want change. This desire for new has been a long time coming, however, and we are pretty backed up.

Unfortunately, we don't understand that this is the case, that we have eons of backed-up feelings and faulty concepts that are rushing to the new, fragile opening, that unexpected thirst for change that is lighting us up from within. We genuinely make a good show of it, and sometimes we take great strides. Until we again find ourselves bogged down, slogging through density and sometimes losing our boots in it. You can hear that wet, sucking sound as we finally get them out and nearly fall over in the process.

What is going on here? Why can't we just steam on forward, giddy in our thirst for life, for ecstatic breath?

The truth? We have lost ourselves again. We have fallen in love with the idea of ourselves, and that must slow us down, dampen our shine. We have forgotten that we are also nobody, and this is what kills us. But not the way that we need to die.

Here's a true story. Someone I knew was killed. Senselessly, or so it appeared. He was a friend, and I grieved. I would pass by his door and be gripped with grief. He didn't deserve to die like that, so violently. Then one day as I passed by his door the now-expected grief welled up in me, and once again I cried. I felt genuine loss and sorrow. But there was also something new, something surprising. It was a simple question: Why am I crying?

It was not a novel question. It was ordinary. And so it stopped me. I let the question do its work, tunneling through me in search of truth, in search of what is real. Several replies presented themselves, but they were tossed to the side like socks with holes in them as I searched for the unholy sock I knew was somewhere in that sock drawer. Eventually I found it, and it was nothing like I knew it would be, nothing like I would have imagined. Even though I knew that sock was in there, which was why I was looking in the first place, now that I had it in front of me I could see very plainly that it didn't belong to me, and that it was the sock I was looking for and that I needed.

I was crying because I was in unreality. I was delusional, believing that my friend, first of all, was gone, and that somehow this death, secondly, was sad. As I drank those truths in, the real kicker landed. My delusion was clearly pathological. That much was now crystal clear. I say this because I uncovered the real reason for my grief. And that was that in a deeper part of myself covered over by defense and conditioning, I believed that this death was about me. That I had been wronged somehow. That *I* didn't deserve it.

And this is always how it goes. We fall in love with an idea of who we are, and then we protect it. To the death. *Everything* becomes about us. In short, we are locked in duality. One hand clapping falling on deaf ears.

What does this have to do with NonDual? It goes to the heart of it. For if we truly wish to understand and experience NonDual Reality, we must eventually turn inward to face death. That is why the best advice to you is to stop this foolishness. Apply yourself to living your life, exactly where and how it is at this moment. It is absolutely perfect. Do not seek NonDual Reality. Let it come to you when you are ready. You definitely have time. Your desire to be better, to have a "more spiritual" life is steeped in your deepest delusions. Best to stop listening to that voice and do what you can to love and help those you love. That is enough. Your "calling" will be your undoing.

However, I understand that it may be too late for that. You have "committed yourself" to your spiritual journey. What this means is that you are headed for deep trouble—if that commitment is indeed real. If not, you have nothing to worry about. You will be protected by your defenses and your delusional self-love to the degree that your path, though possibly bumpy, will be on the whole be an okay ride.

Death, and the study of death, must be your daily medicine if you are not able to turn back from your inquiry into NonDual Reality. And I am not talking about contemplating your own death, for that is too complicated and tricky. There are plenty of other kinds of death to go around before you attempt to be at one with your own death. We should walk before we try to run a steeplechase. In this case, the backdoor approach is best.

Why is this so? Why must death be the topic of study? Because NonDual requires it. To be in your life and simultaneously not be attached to your life is where NonDual Reality resides. Being in your life is already a challenge, but it is an even greater challenge to not be attached to your life, to experience that nothing is really about you in the way that you believe you are. That is the holy grail of NonDual.

3

CHOP WOOD, CARRY WATER

Imagine you are a wildflower, blowing in a spring breeze. That's pretty easy, right? ...Be careful! So quick and you are already in love with yourself as a wildflower. Totally crazy. You have taken your beloved human identity and put the mask of wildflower over it. That alone should alert you to the depth of your self-attachment. Now imagine that you are everything *but* the flower. Much more NonDual.

NonDual is not a thing. It is no-thing.

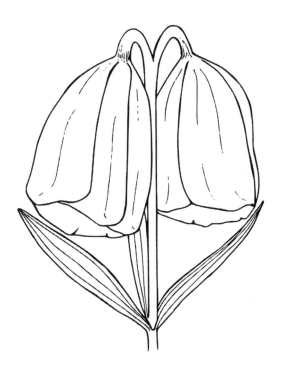

Chopping wood and carrying water means being your self. Giving up grand fantasies about who you could be or would have been and letting your real self have a chance at the wheel. Your real self must always be there, inside of those fantasies, and you are way more than you could ever imagine. That's the important point: you can't imagine your real self. Stop trying to.

Here are two truths: God has a plan. God is the plan. NonDual includes both.

And yes, we need to consider God. God is a stand-in for Oneness, for NonDual. We all personalize God and claim a relationship to God, whether believer, atheist or agnostic. Some seek refuge in NonDual teachings because they do not want to consider God. They have tricked themselves and are now contemplating the navel of God.

Some more fun traps: I am God. I am not God. God loves me. I love God.

These are traps because they make absolutely no sense. There is nothing real there. The first problem of course is "I." Who is that? Or even what is that? Whoever or whatever you think you are, it is a complete fiction. You are not real. Yes, you are interesting, even important, but you cannot be real. What is real does not change, and your idea of who you are changes in each moment. I am hungry. I am not hungry. I am happy. I am not happy.

We are, as you see, pointing at the moon here. Pay no attention to the words. Pay even less attention to the pointing. Your original self is real. No other.

I have another story for you. It is a true story. And it has nothing to do with me. For some time, I believed in myself. Knew that I was a good man with good intentions. I had answers to some of the deepest life questions. It was a good life. I felt content. I had my calling. My favorite stories. I was clear.

But I had stopped reaching into the bottomless pocket to get what I needed. Maybe I even knew that I had stopped. I'm not sure. In any case, I found myself at the end of the road, really nowhere to turn. The road simply stopped, like one of those bridges to nowhere that politicians sometimes build. There was no going forward.

There was no going backward. Both sides were blocked by a sheer wall that I couldn't even grip.

What did I do? I had no choice but to wait. To see what would come next. Or maybe to face the end. I didn't know. What happened next was less of a happening and more of a non-happening. It was extremely ordinary. There were no fireworks, no celebrations that I was invited to.

Eventually, I remembered the bottomless pocket. I was amazed that I could have even forgotten it! How do you forget to breathe? Isn't it automatic? Apparently not. But this time there was a difference. There was no one there to reach into the pocket. That was what had stopped me in the first place, but I didn't know enough to know that.

Revelation #1: I am the bottomless pocket.

That of course is more than a story. It is a treatise on fear. I will do my best to explain.

Fear is the measure of what is not real. The more the fear, the greater the delusion. I know, I know. You have found some exceptions. Fear of heights, you say, is a rational fear. So is fear of fire, and fear of guns, and fear of horrible diseases. You know what? You are correct. These are "healthy" fears, representing actual threats.

But they can never be real. To be real they would need to be permanent, and they are not.

The peace you make with fear, however, is real. It does not go away, even on Sundays. That is because real peace is permanent. Fear may be chronic, ongoing, but it is never permanent.

NonDual Reality is permanent. Non-changing. So no one is there. And that's peaceful, not fearful.

We need to bring this back to the body. How to experience NonDual Reality in the body and not the mind or even the emotions? The answer will surprise you. It is all about not breathing.

As it turns out, we *are* controlling our breathing. The automatic part is buried, like the real self. Shaking ourselves of this false breathing invites NonDual Reality. Truly letting go of our breathing and following it, thoughtless, snaps the controlled breath trance. If it happens even for a moment, that is worth years of practice.

Sorry. You may have noticed that I snuck in "thoughtless." But it is key. Our delusional identity is stitched together with thoughts, as tightly as seams on a baseball. These thoughts are the fabric of our fictional self. No thought. And no breathing. That is the reset button.

But I can't hold my breath! That may be your next thought, your first line of defense. Yet no breathing is not about holding your breath.

They are not the same. What I am referring to happens automatically when you are thoughtless and allow breathing to be whatever it is. Without thought, you are no longer there to control things. The vibration you then feel is "om."

4

FORSAKEN

The most direct and inspirational NonDual teaching in the Christ story comes on the cross. Jesus calls out to God: "Why have you forsaken me?"

This appears on the surface to be full-blown dualistic thinking that stands in stark contrast to Jesus' earlier words that "The Father and I are One."

So what happened? Had Jesus lost his NonDual way?

Doubtful. Given what happens next in the story—resurrection, there is a more plausible explanation. And an invaluable teaching. It has to do with embodying our separate, delusional self.

Acknowledging and bearing witness to our dualistic, separatist self is a requirement for inviting NonDual Reality as an experience.

I have been wary of using the word "witness" thus far because it is a familiar concept in various meditation practices. Bearing witness is much more involved, literally, than the "watching" referred to in witness meditation. You will be mistaken if you equate them. The watching or observing in witness meditation is a precursor, an earlier developmental stage, to bearing witness.

Whether or not you believe Jesus was real, you can learn from this story. Jesus demonstrated the deepest of faith when he allowed himself to embody and bear witness to those remaining separatist, dualistic aspects of himself that became part of his experience on the cross. The full anguish and despair he expressed was a cleansing, a purging of his body of this separatist consciousness.

How does this work? We must start with the understanding that the body is our front row seat to creation in this world. Our alpha point. Time-space is experienced through our body. Our creation begins with the body. We know ourselves as "us" primarily through the body. The boundaries of "I" and "You" as the essential markers of consciousness are demarcated first of all by what is the body and what is not the body.

This means of course that our delusional self, the separated or separatist self, is rooted in the body. Transcending the delusional self occurs through bearing witness to it, which was what Jesus was up to when he cried out about feeling forsaken. And transcending, it must be understood, does not at all mean 'doing away with.' Because this dualistic aspect is not real, there is nowhere for it to go.

The energy that was invested into it gets recycled, returned to its source.

In such a moment like Jesus experienced when he expressed the shadow of his real self, there is little to no room for the witness or observer self. Yet the developmental fruit of witness or observer consciousness, the deepest of faith, is amply present, integrated within the cells of the body and in the overall consciousness of the individual. Expressed fully from the seat of NonDual Reality, the separatist consciousness now finds itself uprooted, held "aloft" in faith. Now it can finally be let go.

Such faith has been built up slowly, perhaps over lifetimes. When it has been sufficiently developed, we can now safely express our deepest anguish and separatist pain without creating more of what is being expressed.

The relativistic or unreal truth of what is being expressed no longer has roots in separatist consciousness (because that consciousness has been replaced by an unspoken and unshakeable faith), and this means that our expression is a clearing out instead of an inviting in.

The key understanding here in this process is that we can't not create. We are always creating. This is how we have been made—in the likeness or image of God. That is our divine identity: a creator being. What Jesus created as the consequence of his expression of despair and anguish was not more separation or delusion but freedom—liberation and resurrection.

The NonDual is well alive in other traditions and teaching as well. In Buddhism, for instance, the cultivation of *nying je chenmo*, or great compassion, is in effect a gateway to NonDual Reality. Opening one's self up to the suffering of others, initially through empathy, breaks through separatist consciousness, the strict attachment to self, and leads eventually to feelings of responsibility toward and for others. From there it is but a short step to the NonDual.

At the foundation of this Buddhist teaching is the warrant or agreement that all sentient beings desire to be free of suffering and to be happy. It is instructive to note that in our opening of ourselves to the suffering of others that we, too, must imagine and therefore experience the other's suffering. The perhaps counter-intuitive consequence is that we work out our own issues in the process, making the practice of compassion something that benefits us directly and immediately, further eroding the delusion of separation.

Hinduism also of course is deeply steeped in NonDual teaching. Brahman, or Ultimate Reality, is the NonDual. From Hinduism and its many gods we get the understanding that God appears to us as reflections of who we are, not as God would or could be in absoluteness. Endowed with form through the many gods, and formless in its transcendent reality, Brahman is Hinduism's way to point at NonDual Reality.

For Islam, the Sufi poet Rumi speaks repeatedly of NonDual Reality. He writes:

Why should I seek?
I am the same as he.
His essence speaks through me.
I have been looking for myself.

The NonDual, as we see, is right in front of us, taught by all the major religions of the world. Why, then, does it remain invisible?

We are blind, following stories that are not based in reality.

5

THE EMPEROR'S CLOTHES

Perpetuating mass delusion is the game of kings and those who attend them, as the children's story shows us. Once again, it is the child who shows the way.

But do you want children running things? I do not. The child as the answer is itself a prevailing delusion. This particular fantasy tries to suggest that we have lost something behind us in time, and that we need to go back and get it. Ha! Go for it. Tell us how it goes. Last time I looked, time was a one-way street going somewhere in a real hurry.

Here's the rub: we need to manage the truth of NonDual Reality within the framework or dynamic model of evolution. Like a holographic gyroscope seeking true north—anything thing else throws it way off kilter so that it becomes deadly.

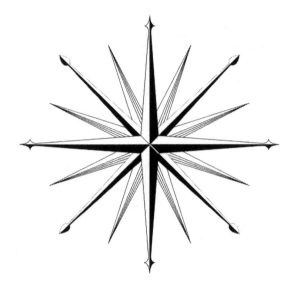

What does this tell us right away? That we have no real use for kings. Or queens. NonDual Reality does not discriminate. In fact, placing others above or below us demonstrates that we have not the first clue about reality.

Yet clearly there are stages of development. Evolution is evident all around us. Children and adults, and everything in between. And there are also abundant examples all around us of people getting stuck in a stage of development.

Entire countries getting stuck. Even humanity as a whole.

Our current global crisis, in fact—global warming, economic globalism, global toxicity—is evidence that we are stuck in the evolutionary transition from reductionist hierarchy to nested holism. From me to we.

But 'stuck' is not the right word. It suggests that something is wrong. Actually, we are stuck and simultaneously not stuck. NonDual is both/ and. Keeping this top of mind keeps our gyroscope on track.

Going for true north, moving into "we," requires compassion. It requires greater understanding and acceptance of NonDual Reality, a phrase which is of course redundant. Reality, by its very nature, is NonDual. Nonetheless, we must use NonDual Reality until we have reached a tipping point and there are commercials for NonDual toothpaste and NonDual motorcycles. That will mean we have found ourselves.

Yet everything that is happening, all of our personal and global crises, is required. It is what we need, even when we do not want it or know even that we need it. Some call it a birth, this move from "me" to "we." Painful and necessary for what comes next.

Yet it is more than birth. It is also death. Birth and death are dualistic conceptions for the ongoing evolutionary process of transcendence, the trajectory into the unknown. They are concepts for moving into a new form while bringing the old form along with us to be added to, expanded upon, renewed—all from the inside out.

The difficulty is to hold the NonDual and evolution at the same time. NonDual assures us that all is well, while evolution demands that we face our current "problem" and move beyond it, transcend it. This is both universal and intimately personal.

What compounds the difficulty is teleological thinking, which is so natural to evolutionary thought. The false belief here is that there is "somewhere" to go, some goal that is final. Seeing NonDual as a goal is to misapprehend NonDual.

We must therefore stop making an endpoint out of NonDual, for we are distorting it beyond recognition. And the basic problem in this regard is that when we see NonDual Reality or Oneness as the goal, we will never arrive. We will continue getting halfway there, for eternity. That is because we are using the mind to try and figure this thing out, but the mind is a categorizing tool that needs something else—

imagination and faith perhaps—to let go into transcendence.

Yet there is of course a way, and it is gracefully obvious. The only way out of this apparent paradox between NonDual and teleological evolutionary drive is to embrace and become friends with Mystery. We must allow ourselves infinite surprise. This is due to the fact that we will never be in charge, never be able to control our experience. Such capacity will forever stay out of reach, an actualized Zeno paradox.

It must be enough that we can navigate our choices through the understanding of what is real. For this we can use the two essential framings of our experience: Inside/Outside and Same/Different. Used wisely, they will always point to the NonDual.

Inside/Outside and Same/Different are the orienting frames for our experience of being consciously alive. Starting with the body, we orient ourselves with the perspectives of inside and outside. It is of course a real trick, an amazing sleight of hand, because there is nothing in our experience that is actually outside. We just pretend that there is.

All experience is interior. What we see may in fact be outside, but the experience will always be interior since our vision is —as are all senses— essentially internal. The senses are part of the body, therefore interior. We can only *imagine* external, not ever experience it. Intriguingly, then, our shorthand for *other* is 'outside' or 'external.' Anything and everything that is not "me" is *other* or external/outside.

Don't skip over this, thinking it is too simple, too obvious. There is much more here to unpack. When we make the connection that inside and outside equate to self and other, we have laid the foundation for the next step: understanding that our interior experience is also "other" in the sense that we are observing or witnessing it. Our most intimate interior, our awareness, makes "other" of our experience, which is of course also interior.

What, then, is exterior or external? Anything at all? And who, then, is the watcher? We are so familiar with it/him/her that we assume that it is us, that it is who I am, who you are.

What if we are both wrong and right about this?

To sum up: We are "other" to ourselves. It can be no other way. Consciousness demands it. To have a subject, I, there must me an object, you. Or, alternately, an object, me.

We are skirting the boundaries of the NonDual, where you are a fiction. As am I.

But first, what about same/different? The orientation frames offered here are inside/outside and same/different. This is how we navigate the seemingly mismatched truths of NonDual and evolution.

Inside and outside, or interior and exterior, are very much different than we thought. Exterior can never be an experience. We also make our own experience an "other."

We are even having some real doubts perhaps about "who" we really are.

Same and different is the next navigating frame to consider. Compare and contrast. This is what we do *all* the time. For practical reasons, we need to know that a shoe is not an automobile. We also need to know that an apple will always look like other apples. We make "sense" of the world and our experience this way.

In noticing and sorting for same and different, we have the basic knowledge to make choices about what we prefer. That's the point. It's all about what we prefer, what we like, which is simultaneously about what we don't like. Same and different.

I like this, but I don't like that. I am this way, but I am not that way. You like this, but you do not like that. You are this way, but you are not that way.

As I claimed earlier, this is how we navigate our experience and make choices: with inside / outside (self / other) and same / different.

The trouble begins, though, when we try to establish who we are to start with. And this is what's taking us up to the door of the NonDual.

6

BE STILL AND KNOW GOD

When your mind is quiet, no thought, who are you?

Better yet: When your mind is quiet, no thought, do you even care who you are?

All of these preferences that you have collected, are they real? Some, no doubt, are very real. And others are easily abandoned, left on the curb without a second thought.

When we defend our preferences, we are in delusion. The reason for this is that what is true, what is real, needs no defense. And the real you can never be defended because there is nothing "there" to defend.

That is the secret to beginner's mind.

Mystery. Eternal surprise. What is real is understood to be real, and all else is a display of similar and different—both inside and outside. It is a pageantry of possibility.

To try is to be delusional. Psychotic even.

Let's see if we can discern between our two basic selves. There is first of all the I/me that we know so well. The "I" here is the watcher, the awareness. "Me" is what we identify as who we are, our preferences.

I/me is the fictional self. It exists. Very much so. But it is not real. We are attached to this version of our consciousness. We like it. We love it even. Yet we also hate it. We must hate it because it is not real. And that internal experience of hate that we sometimes ascribe to external others, it is of course not them. It is us. We are hating ourselves, but we will not allow that. It violates our delusional, separatist self-love. So we delude ourselves into believing that it is the "other" that we hate for causing these feelings in us that we hate. We are in this way very much insane.

It's also important for you to know that if you believe you do not hate, you are deeply delusional. And you harbor a hidden killer. The sooner you invite him or her to dinner with you, the better.

The other self is I/we. No, this is not NonDual. But operating from this self may encourage NonDual Reality to stop in for a visit.

I/we is not better than I/me. Both are necessary.

I/we acknowledges that you are capable of feeling anything and everything that anyone else has ever felt or will feel. The best and the worst. I/we is therefore born out of empathy, compassion and joy. In I/we, we are still fully ourselves, sanely individuated, and we are also correctly placed in the "other." In I/we, we understand that everyone, all sentient beings, share the same watcher, and we are not disturbed or concerned about this. It is a delight. We accept the rightfulness of our place in the order of the universe. In God's plan even.

So what about God?

When we are still, truly still, we are knowing God. There is, however, much unlearning to be done before this is possible. It is unlearning because nothing can be added to truth. Anything added is delusion. This does not make it wrong. We must go through delusion to get anywhere worth going. Delusion shows us the way. Take away delusion, and you are standing in reality.

How do we know if we are in delusion? Ask yourself: I/me or I/we? If you are honest, you will immediately know if you are in delusion. Which does not mean that the delusion will immediately drop away. Probably not, in fact. We love our delusions, and we do not give up what we love without a fight. I/me is the most compelling story you have ever told yourself. So much juicy drama and heroic struggle. It's tough to take off the cape.

We can, however, prepare the ground. We can practice reality. But we cannot practice NonDual. That makes no sense.

One way to practice reality is to allow motion to inside/outside. Nothing, after all, is unmoving when we are in time-space. Everything is in constant play and display. So we can track what is coming in, and what is going out. Taking in and giving out.

We must know that we are talking about Giving and Receiving. This is the play, the display of who we are—both in and out of reality. It is an intimate part of who we are.

We can start here with gratitude. Gratitude, when you see it through the lens of Giving and Receiving, is "coming in." We perceive gratitude as an influx of positive feelings of appreciation. We feel the warmth build up in us as we give our attention to those people and things that we are grateful for. We are receiving that precious energy of gratitude.

Next, we can deepen this. We can acknowledge that we are worthy of these feelings, of this energy.

We can allow even more building up or acknowledgment of these feelings by entertaining the idea that we actually deserve and are worthy of what we appreciate. Inherently worthy, that is. Not because we have done anything to deserve what we are grateful for.

Accepting and receiving our inherent worthiness may not always be possible. We may resist it, and this will stop us from feeling or perceiving the flowing in of positive feelings and energy, of love. What is happening is that we are stuck in I/me. We believe there is a story here to be defended, something to justify the separatist identity. It is a fiction, this self, but it exists. We can now directly observe how our separatist identity, our identification with and love for a delusional story, stops our flow of positivity.

We may even be ready here to defend our delusional self *to the death* because we are *that* certain that we are not worthy. So, to be honest with ourselves, to be in integrity, we refuse to acknowledge our inherent worth. We are stubbornly and militantly denying our basic worth while tricking ourselves into believing that we are doing it to be in integrity, to uphold the truth. We feel noble about it even.

Can you see how crazy that is? How I/me can twist things around in absurd ways so that the fiction may continue? And we actually fall for it. Again and again. For lifetimes even.

Once we have experienced a measure of worthiness for what supports us and for what we appreciate and love, we may now allow some Giving as part of our practice. We have allowed enough positivity to move inward, and we can feel it. This means that we can now start Giving by giving inner voice to what we wish to praise or celebrate. Our actions and our words can be praise and celebration, and so can our inner imagining. The words "I love" and "I appreciate" are setting things up for that giving of praise. We can feel positivity within us grow or strengthen as we make these inner or even spoken statements of praise and celebration.

The next step is to deepen the Giving. We do this with compassion and its twin sibling forgiveness. We can literally reach out with our giving by feeling compassion and forgiveness to others. It's best to imagine, to picture, specific others. Both those who are suffering greatly at the moment as well as those whom we believe have harmed us cruelly and unfairly. We are giving out of the pool of our gratitude and worthiness, and this pool, we realize, is infinitely deep.

Notice that we have given to ourselves first. Otherwise, we cannot last. If we do not feel charged up with positivity, there is no way that we can really give. If we try, we will be taking, not giving.

There is one last step to our practice, and it takes us right up to the threshold of Nondual. This step is to now enter into trust.

Trust is both giving and receiving. We experience a letting go, a falling in to trust that opens the gates of positivity to flow in, yet we are also stepping forward to trust, which is giving. This is why trust takes us right up to the door of the NonDual.

And trust is of course another name for faith. Faith is difficult for some of us because we confuse faith with religious dogma, but trust is something we can understand and accept.

To truly practice trust, we need to take on our biggest worries, our biggest concerns and make the choice of trust. If we need to start with hope, that is perfectly fine. Hope is unripe faith. And hope can only ever develop into trust or faith with practice, so it is wonderful to bring hope to our biggest worries and concerns—and this goes much better if we first of all practice the preparatory steps of gratitude, worthiness, praise and compassion.

Why this practice? Is it necessary? No. It may, however, tune us up some and develop our sensitivities for the building blocks of NonDual Reality: Give and Take, You and I, Yes and No.

7

Unmasking Fear

What fuels the separatist self, the I/me? Fear.

That is the food it requires to survive. All the justifications and stories that we use to defend our delusions are designed by the brilliance of the I/me consciousness. I/me is a genius; of this there is no doubt. And that cleverness, that ingenuity, stems from the fact that the separatist self is grounded in and dependent upon what is real. That is the source of its genius. Nothing can ever be truly separate from NonDual Reality.

Our delusions are unbelievably convincing and persuasive. That is because they are like a mobius strip, turning things inside out in ways that we don't catch on to very easily. Even when we question things, aware on some level that we are being had, we don't catch the twists. We are too close to them. We have accepted too many of them for too long. They have become the air we breathe.

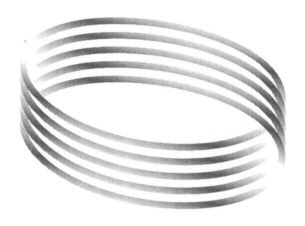

Here's a simple question to prove the point. Answer right away, automatically. Q: How many sides to a coin?

Of course everyone knows that there are two sides to a coin, and of course everyone is wrong. It's a delusion in plain sight. The reality is that nothing in our 3-dimensional existence can have only 2 sides. Three is the absolute minimum. This is so obvious, but we miss such things all the time—especially when they support our most beloved delusion: I/me.

Fear is usually what compels us to abandon any doubts about this fiction we are so invested in. Fear twists us into accepting ridiculous paradox, into circular reasoning that is so subtle that we completely miss it. Over time, we become so used to the delusions that we become complacent. We believe we know how things go, so we stop questioning. Of course. There are two sides to a coin. And that is where we create more suffering.

To stay awake to the reality of I/we, we need to keep in mind that our I/me consciousness, our most prevalent delusion, is kept operative, kept alive, by fear. It's not difficult to see how this works. We separate ourselves, we pull back, out of fear. I/me is the "wise" voice within us, counseling us on what and whom to watch out for. That is because fear is the operating system of I/me, of separatist consciousness. If there is no fear, there is no I/me.

Everybody knows this about fear, that fear keeps us down. And down and out. Yet we also have this story going that tells us that fear is what keeps us safe, that there is of course something we can call healthy fear. Without fear, our argument goes, we would hurt ourselves by taking outrageous or even not-so-outrageous risks. It is, after all, a dangerous world.

So let's play devil's advocate with this. Let's entertain our strongest critics. There is absolutely nothing to fear (!) about doing this because we will welcome any shedding of untruth that such an encounter may bring.

We need to start with the toughest critic of all: the truth that we live in a world of fantastic beauty—and horrific suffering. There is nothing at all "unreal" about the suffering in our world.

War, murder, human trafficking, rape, and all the myriad forms of abuse that are limited only by human imagination. That, this position holds, is the unfortunate reality of life on earth. And because this is so, fear has a rightful place in our lives. Asking us to live without fear is irresponsible and just plain wrong.

Pretty convincing, right? The argument is difficult, even impossible, to counter. Healthy fear keeps us alive and others safe. We need fear.

Perhaps you are right. Perhaps I have painted myself into a corner here—though I never claimed that we do not need fear or even that we can do away with it. But allow me nonetheless to give this my best shot.

There is nothing wrong with fear. As pointed out, fear has a practical purpose that keeps us from harming ourselves and being harmed. Fear alerts us, in fact, to the presence of pending pain—real and imagined. We must therefore stay attuned to our fears, for they will both keep us safe and teach us about our I/me operations. Where there is fear, there is separation. And separation is the grand delusion. It follows, therefore, that we need to make friends with fear because fear will point directly at where we are defending the indefensible. Fear highlights our pointless worry, fear reveals our psychotic doubt, and fear alerts us to our falseness, to our phony pretenses.

But fear, as our critic so correctly assumes, cannot be dropped overnight. It would be ludicrous to suddenly start pretending that we are without fear. NonDual Reality, however, remains the bedrock of truth. So what to do? Invite fear in. Pretending it away or blocking fear will only compound the delusion. That's because the truth always shakes off what is untrue. It may take awhile, and it may lead to our physical death, but truth cannot be denied because it is by definition the fabric of what is real.

There is no greater gold mine for finding the real self than in the mines of fear. This is because fear is the inverse of what is real. Fear assumes separation. NonDual Reality abides in complete wholeness. That is why we can correctly assert that where there is no fear, there is no I/me.

Fear holds a further gift for us as well. Fear, like its opposite—faith, is simultaneously inwardly and outwardly moving. With faith, you may recall, we experience this as an allowing, an inward movement, and also a stepping forward, an outward moving. Faith is a peaceful, nourishing experience. Fear, however, holds the container for two seemingly destructive forces—rage and despair. This is why we are sometimes angry when we are afraid, and sometimes we feel sad when afraid. The truth here, however, is that wherever there is rage, there is despair, and wherever there is despair, rage also lives.

Why are these forces only "seemingly" destructive? Because you cannot destroy what is real, what abides. Rage and despair, the most destructive of human forces, cause great, great suffering and pain. This is nothing to take lightly. This is why pretending to not have these forces within us is very unwise, though quite common. Would you rather know that you have a rattlesnake in your basement, or would you prefer to not know?

With NonDual Reality, there is no judgment of these destructive forces. They are understood to be necessary in the evolutionary development of our souls. To reveal truth, divine law unleashes "the slings and arrows of outrageous fortune" as well as "mighty blows of fate" until "at long last those blows ... teach us wisdom." As Shakespeare and Sophocles tell us, it is, without question, a painful journey.

This is precisely why fear is so important. There is no better guide to our potentials for love, creativity and fulfillment. Like Jesus' cry of despair on the cross, we are well advised to become intimate with our fears and to express the rage and despair that they harbor—to bear witness and be freed.

8

THE PARADOX OF SELF LOVE

From the NonDual perspective, self love is extremely interesting. Think about it. The Universal Self is active in each of us, yet we are also individuated consciousnesses. We are simultaneously All That Is and Just Me, I/we and I/me. So what does it actually mean, to love one's self?

It quickly gets rather complicated. Which "I" am I talking about? How do I differentiate "me"?

It's not unreasonable to even consider the possibility that self love is an impossibility, like seeing your own eyeballs or biting your own teeth. That there is no way to get a clear sense of an "I" that loves a "me."

"I love you" is much, much easier. The "I" and "you" are represented by different bodies, different histories, different personalities. So, can we get a clear sense of "me" by how others see us? In part, yes. We do it all the time when we learn about ourselves through others' responses to us. Yet we also seem to have a definite sense of who we are regardless of how others see us and interact with us. This seems to be where we should concentrate our search for a "me" that we can love.

Generally speaking, both "I" and "me" are represented by the same body, right? This is where we have the first challenge. We quickly must conclude therefore that neither "I" nor "me" is something completely tangible— something less clear and in fact not true at all at times when we are considering "you" and "others." When we say, for example, "I love myself," the "self" is not necessarily physical— though we do say that we love our hair or our eyes or our hands and other physical aspects of our selves.

In short, we see our "selves" as both physical and nonphysical, but when we say "I love myself" we may be including the body but are often more tuned in to something else, some intangible yet seemingly definite self that we identify with perhaps analogously to how we identify with our bodies.

In fact, we can return to our orientation of inside/outside and same/different to guide us. Our bodies are understood and somehow experienced or imagined as external, which do allow them to sort of be an "other" as we discovered earlier. At the same time, we do identify with them—extremely in fact—as "me," which includes interiority, our internal being.

To get more quickly to where this discussion is going and to what matters in the context of NonDual Reality, let's accept that we are pretty much on track here—at least as far as the "me" goes. We sanely see that our "self" is physical and non-physical, inside and outside. Our "I," however, is a bit trickier.

Because we generally do not see mind as physical in any way, that is we mostly or nearly always identify "I" as something intangible and related to or identifiable as mind, the only location we have for "I," the only address, is interior.

So let's keep things straight:

"Me" can be interior and exterior, but "I" is interior only.

Exterior is perceived as other, except for one's own physical body—which is exterior but also at least conceived of as or identified with interior. We may in fact simultaneously experience interior and exterior with our own bodies.

Exterior is perceived of as outside of us, yet all of our experiences of exterior are interior experiences – except for the body, which is both. Seemingly, we cannot experience exterior in an absolute way because there is no "I" there.

And what can we draw from all of this relatively obvious stuff that we rarely consider? That we identify an "I" that is interior only, and that the only relatively complete experience we have of inside/outside is through our own bodies.

Put in perhaps straighter terms, we are well advised to be wary of "I" as a measure of reality (since it has no exterior that we can identify and is therefore not whole), and well advised to bring much more attention to our sense of self as expressed through and with our bodies, our "me."

This becomes *extremely* interesting when looked at through the lens of NonDual Reality. "I" is very tricky, "me" not so much. As a separated self, an individuated self, I/me makes sense. It works. It's only when we start exploring and examining the "I" that it stops making sense.

So check out this idea: NonDual is NonSense. By that I mean that when we start considering I/we as a perspective, an identification even, we begin to lose sense of ourselves, our "me."

And it's precisely here where we begin to spin out, to start tripping over ourselves as we attempt to explain and grasp NonDual Reality. But we have found the key. It is "I."

More specifically, "I Am." "I Am" represents the Universal Self, God. Notice that there is no "me" here and no "you" here. "Me" and "You" reflect "I Am," and as such they are not "I Am" in the absolute sense. But without "me" and "you" we cannot know God. In fact, we can't know anything really because knowing requires reflection. It also requires memory. And the comparisons wrought by mystery and knowing that we call imagination.

We say God is Love because that's the closest we can get as conscious, aware beings who know things to the truth of God. Love integrates and includes "I" and "you" or interior/exterior and same/different. Love accepts and appreciates all, and gives and receives from that complete, unconditional acceptance and appreciation.

The hangup of course is that we have multiple "I"s. We have I/me, and we have I/we.

It's easy to blame our troubles, our suffering, on I/me. And that attribution is correct, but not in the condemning way of blame. There is no victim, no perpetrator in NonDual Reality. Responsible is a better word here. I/me is definitely the source of our ills because it is not real. It is a fiction that runs counter to the truth of I/we. It is of course a deadly fiction.

But there is absolutely nothing wrong with I/me. It is necessary for our development, for our becoming. As we realized earlier, we need I/me to have an understanding of wholism, of being holy. It is in "me" that we experience interior/exterior simultaneously, that we marry subject and object and witness it intimately.

For our development, for our evolution into those who intimately know God, we actually need to get down and dirty with "me." Our bodies are the closest we can get to knowing anything real, and this includes NonDual Reality. This may be exactly the opposite of what you have been imagining about NonDual Reality, that it is somehow 'out there' instead of both 'out there' and 'in here,' which only the body can provide.

Body First must be our mantra if we desire to be present, still, and know God.

9

THY WILL BE DONE

What is God's will? From the perspective of NonDual Reality, of Holiness, God's will is everything that happens. This may be a problematic understanding from the I/me view that sees God's will as only what is good. God's will, this view holds, cannot include evil. From the I/me perspective, the very idea that evil is contained within God is complete insanity. Probably enough to go to war over.

This perspective remains prevalent because it can be difficult to hold a static notion of truth/untruth while simultaneously allowing for dynamic development—in addition to acknowledging the two "I"s of I/me and I/we. In fact as long as there is a perception of evil as external and something to be negated or denied internally, the I/we perspective will be challenging or unavailable. The paradox of God containing evil may be too much for the I/me that struggles to do what is right and atone for doing what is wrong.

The larger issue here of course is will. "Thy will and not my will" is a common expression of humility and piety, and it's definitely in line with static ideas of I/me. However, adding evolution or development into the picture suggests something more along the lines of "My will to become Thy will." This conception allows for the fact that our choices are gradually and inevitably going to evolve from the I/me perspective to the reality of I/we. That, one could say, is God's will and God's plan.

We can go no further without understanding, at least in broad strokes, the birth, the genesis, of I/me. As the identification with the delusion of separation, I/me is created out of an experience that is interpreted as separation. The response to that experience is born out of the desire to survive and avoid annihilation and creates a separate identity, the I/me. It is primarily a defense against the feelings brought about in the separation experience and an offense, a forward-moving intention, to prevent that or similar experiences from ever happening again.

I/me is self-recreating. Its defensive and offensive moves create exactly what it wishes to avoid— more feelings and experiences of separation. This doubles down the efforts, solidifying the I/me as the viable identity. Soon enough, this fiction, this delusion, is accepted as reality.

We are not done with will yet, however, because will holds an important key. The original experience that was interpreted as separation is referred to by many as The Fall, and in this story we see that the separation was a choice, an expression of free will. As individuated consciousnesses, we each have the right and capacity to choose the truth of reality or indeed to choose something else. To the degree that we identify with I/me, we are choosing the delusion of separation. God, as Love, as NonDual Reality, must accept our choice. NonReality, however, abides, and we will eventually find our way back to reality through our search for Wholeness, Holiness—the domain of God.

How? Seriously, how do we ever get out of our delusion? The answer is surprisingly simple: we create our way out by reaching again and again into the bottomless pocket of our being to once again align ourselves and our choices with what is true, real, and right. With Love.

Another way to grasp this is to reconsider the teaching mentioned earlier that we are made in the image of God. The image, or reflection, of God. As such, we must create. We always create and create on all levels of our being at all times. Our doubts create. Our fears create. Our positivity creates. Everything creates. Consciousness creates.

There are some who claim that our entire world, our experiences in the time-space continuum, is created by our collective will to find holiness.

NonDual Reality abides. It is all-accepting. This understanding gives us more clues for us to recognize our own delusions and accept them. Not judge them. Judging in the sense of desiring to destroy or negate our delusions is definitely I/me in action.

Primarily, we must, as discussed earlier, live with our delusions in our bodies. Bear witness to them as Jesus showed us on the cross. This will naturally unwind the defenses and offenses that perpetuate our suffering.

In the end, we will discover that our primary experience of delusion, under all the covers, is shame. Why is this? Because all other bad feelings and unhappiness are overtly causal or conditional. I'm unhappy because of this or that. I'm feeling bad right now while I'm waiting for my test results. Whatever. In fact, even shame is causal, but we generally don't see it that way because we don't fully understand yet that our beliefs are creating our experience. And the belief of shame is very clear: I am unworthy. This belief can be formed in many ways, such as "I am not enough" or "I am despicable" —or any number of variations on this basic theme. Of course seeing others as unworthy is also a convenient cover for our own insecurities and shame.

In some part of our being we will always know the truth. There can never be full separation, never be a full break from NonDual Reality. This friction we feel between our delusion and the truth of what is real, this uneasiness and anxiety, will never leave us until we have found what it takes to bear witness to our shame. "Why Have You Forsaken Me?"

And there may be many layers here: guilt may unfold to shame, anger may unfold to shame, fear may unfold to shame. Eventually we must find ways to be compassionate with our delusional I/me and heal. Acceptance is step one, and bearing witness will follow.

But here's the question we all ask at some point: Can we experience I/we in our bodies? Can we be I/me and I/we simultaneously?

Of course. NonDual Reality is the most ordinary truth, so it is available to us. We know it when we experience it because we are Inside

AND Outside, Same AND Different. And we recognize the feeling of NonDual Reality because it is the foundation of being, which is Love.

Excerpt from Book II of The Nonsense of NonDual: In the Mind of God

1. The Real You

In the mind of God, the story of the real you is written in the most precious light of love. In this story, the only true story about you, everything about your life—including your struggles, your pain, and your quite possibly deeply hidden confusion about who you really are, is exactly as it should be. And if—and this is of course a very big (perhaps the biggest) if—we were able to see and experience ourselves in and through the mind of God, we would know and experience such a complete approval and praise of our being that all those pains and discomforts would be impossible to even imagine. Completely impossible.

It's important to understand this before we take on the challenge of exploring what "the mind of

God" even means. That is because the big takeaway here is that the usual story of who we are that we go around telling to ourselves and to others is not real. The experience of that separate self is of course very real in a sensory sense, but the story itself is bogus. It is a fiction, a sometimes almost unrecognizable version of the real story, the real you.

It is remarkable that we are in fact so used to our fictional story that we rarely question it. And I say "in fact" because that's how we tend to treat this story—even as we change it. We treat it as fact. This is precisely how we end up feeling so secure about the collection of half-truths, rationalizations and deflections that make up so much of our cherished fictional self. We declare the story to be "factual," and this gives us something to lean on, something to feel secure in. Mind, as it must, charms us into believing our own propaganda, good and bad.

But the mind of God? I can almost hear you say it: "Are you kidding?" How could there be a mind of God? Isn't "mind" just more duplicitous duality? Doesn't "mind" come with separation—a separate subject and a separate object? And therefore our suffering, our exasperating and painful struggle to be free? How could there be, in this and in any case, the mind of God? Isn't mind "the problem"?

You are right of course. And you are also mistaken. That is largely because the crazy thing about the word "mind" is that we really don't know what we are talking about when we use it! We can't! And that makes it perfect for talking about God. The essential problem (if we want to label it a problem) is that when we talk or think or feel into the meaning of "mind," we must use our minds to do it. How lovely! Like a cartoon character running wildly from some unnameable danger, we have crashed through the wall of the most confounding question, leaving just the dark shape of where we disappeared into territory we cannot imagine nor find words for. We have, to state it simply, run into the most important, potentially show-stopping question: Metaphorically speaking, can we see our own eyes? Can we possibly know about the mind of God when we must use our own mind to know it? Can we even know *if* there is a mind of God?

Are you a little confused yet? Disoriented? I hope so. To entertain this idea of "the mind of God," we must leave our knowing mind behind. The mind of God cannot be what we think.

Please consider what I am pointing to. There is a very good explanation for why we are often so stuck, so entranced by the fiction of our separate self. And that is this: the separate, unreal self is totally addicted to knowing. The worst addict ever, in fact. The original, archetypal addict. The Adam & Eve of all addicts. Try as we might, the mind of God is not about knowing, so you will not be able to know it in the normal ways of knowing.

The only thing that makes sense about the mind of God is that you cannot know it.

You can also never learn anything that is real. At least not in the usual sense of "learn." The reason for that is because what is real, what is true, is what remains when all that is untrue has been cleared away. Adding information or understanding will not help our quest for the experience of what is real, of nondual reality. What is real, abides, unchanging. It cannot be added to in any way. It is the only number that when you add zero to it, you get zero, not the number.

I am using too many words to get this across to you, so I will take another approach. I will trick your mind into believing you have learned something new, something valuable. Forgive me for this. Later you will smile, maybe laugh out loud and want to call me on the phone to laugh with me. Perhaps we will meet for kombucha.

It has already happened. Did you get it? I got you, if only slightly and half-heartedly, to imagine a pleasant experience in the future— when you had grasped some great truth—but the truth is that everything was all in your mind. We never left the moment. There is no future. And that is mind.

Twice! Did you get it?? I'm really hoping that at least the second one worked. When you thought I was talking about and explaining the first trick, I was actually using a second trick, the one that mattered. Distracting you so that I could say what mattered when you were not expecting it. Demonstrating mind.

Mind is the most slippery substance ever invented. So slippery that we need to trick our minds to glimpse it just as it finishes running right through our fingers. It's probable in fact that you only think that you *might* have seen it.

Here's the deal. The mind as we generally know it, the dualistic mind, is all about knowing. What this mind, however, cannot understand, is that what it truly craves is not-knowing. It can't know this because that would be the end of it. It would take the last bus and never be seen or heard from again. And that's not how mind sees or imagines itself. The mind would never knowingly take the bus in a graceful exit.

Actually, it *could* not. We need to trick it. Pack a nice lunch and convince it that the bus is taking us to the airport for our exotic vacation. We can make nice later. And we will want to. Mind is not bad. Mind is just mind. And very useful, something we don't really want to lose.

Telling mind that it can't know itself is like telling a philosopher that the goal of philosophy is silence. It's likely that it won't go well. What, it/she/he wonders, will there be to do? Where will I put all my words, all my stories? What about our lunch date on the bus?

As you no doubt know, the separate, dualistic mind is the author of the fictional self. Don't get me wrong—mind will be happy to change its story to whatever you want if it thinks that's what will work to stay in control and for you to keep feeding it this way. And it'll do so in a flash—so quickly that you'll never notice. But what our dualistic mind can't do is not have a story. For that, we need the mind of God.

******

WOULD YOU LIKE A FREE GIFT?

Please visit
www.TheNonSenseOfNonDual.com/gift.

Thank you.

ABOUT THE AUTHOR

Liam Quirk is a writer, teacher, singer-songwriter and Pathwork Teacher. His interest in NonDual Reality was sparked by experiences with Zen meditation in 1980. He understands that he is also a complete fiction.

You may contact Liam through email:
Liam@TheNonSenseofNonDual.com

NOTES: